Bygone Da
In the Northern Derbyshire Dales

Lindsey Porter

The Horizon Press

Published by
Horizon Editions Ltd,
Trading as The Horizon Press
The Oaks, Moor Farm Road West, Ashbourne, DE6 1HD
Tel: (01335) 347349
books@thehorizonpress.co.uk

1st Edition

ISBN 978-1-84306-528-9

 British Library Cataloguing in Publication Data: a catalogue record for this book is available from the British Library.

Print: Gomer Press, Llandysul, Ceredigion, Wales

Front cover: Derwent Hall Youth Hostel and bridge

Back cover: The *Spar Queen*

page 1: The former Edensor Inn at Chatsworth Park. It is now the Estate Office

Acknowledgements

The author wishes to acknowledge the assistance received from The YHA,
Mrs L Baggaley, G Ellis, J Alcock, J Brocklebank, the late JA Fleming, Diane Naylor and A Scrivener.
I wish to thank all those who have helped me with images over the years.

CONTENTS

INTRODUCTION

This book is a companion volume to my Southern Derbyshire Dales printed in September 2010. Including some photographs I published 26 years ago, there are also some really interesting scenes of Derwent Hall and the village of Derwent in the 1940s, prior to flooding by Ladybower Reservoir.

Other new ones, previously unpublished, include Ashford Mill, now largely demolished for road widening of the A6 and a photograph of the Fernilee Reservoir suspension bridge. I have been looking for one of this since 1978, having walked across it in c. 1960. Finally one turned up in 2009, along with a photograph of Errwood Farm youth hostel, which was one of the initial eleven opened at Easter 1931.

There are others and I have included some interesting scenes in Buxton, especially one taken prior to 1901 from the rear of the Town Hall looking towards The Crescent and beyond. The images herein cover the area from an imaginary line from Buxton to Bakewell, north to the Woodlands area of the River Derwent (around the Ladybower Reservoir) and Longdendale.

Old scenes give us a good insight into how our parents and grandparents used to live. In many cases, they reflect a way of life long since gone and now largely forgotten. The photographs I have selected hopefully together reflect what the Dales were like in days gone by. I have used a few and only a few, images out of the county where they tie in well with what did exist in the Dales, or where the Dales just happen to fall just outside the county boundary.

To compliment this book and *Bygone Days in the Southern Derbyshire Dales* will be *Visiting Britain's Heritage*: *The Peak District*. This looks at buildings and other features, such as a few archaeological sites and even a few customs which survive. Our local heritage is a rich one and I hope this new book will also appeal to you, combing lots of illustrations and hopefully, an informative text.

What old photographs do not do is describe what life was like on a day to day basis. Horizon will be publishing before Christmas 2010 '*Memories of a Moorland Farmer*', which describes life on a Staffordshire Moorlands hill farm situated close to the former Mermaid Inn, on Morridge. This book, well illustrated with contemporary photographs, portrays the difficulties experienced by hill farmers far better than any photograph can. It certainly describes a way of life which has gone, one which we have difficulty comprehending today. It was written by the late Len Ward, who featured in a BBC TV programme 'Living on the Land' in the 1970s. Hannah Huxley from Yorkshire may be remembered as being another person portrayed at that time.

I do hope that you like the selection of photographs reproduced in this book.

Lindsey Porter
Ashbourne 2010

Ashford

Ashford Mill was well known in Victorian times, and even much earlier, for the production of polished Derbyshire and also Black 'marble'. It was powered by possibly three waterwheels, one of which may be seen here. A few of the buildings remain, but most were lost to road widening in the early 1930s. Many items made here may be seen in the county's churches and country houses. The mill started in 1748 and closed in 1905.

Ashopton

This village existed where the river Derwent was crossed by the Glossop to Sheffield road and is now submerged below Ladybower Reservoir. Here is Cox Bridge, where the road crossed the river. Apparently no remains of the village can be seen by divers: all is covered with sediment. See also pp23-30.

This railway bridge was built to carry the railway built from near Bamford to the Derwent and Howden dams. Millions of tons of stone was brought this way for the construction work. Although a poor image, the bridge in the foreground is Cox Bridge also seen in the photograph above.

Bakewell

These premises in Bath Street were demolished in 1890 to make way for a new Town Hall. The bath was in the old town house of the Duke of Rutland, now on the corner of Bath Gardens. It was a huge thing using thermal water. However hopes of developing Bakewell as a spa never materialised.

Twin waterwheels at the DP Battery Works by the A6. These were painted in 1905. Notice the penstock carrying water to the lower wheel curving around the higher wheel. Such an arrangement was unusual.

The Bakewell sheep dip adjacent to Holme bridge. It still survives but probably has not been used for its true purpose for decades.

Bakewell Station gaily decorated for perhaps a royal visitor. The stone-built station survives, but of course the line has gone.

The station staff of 18 people with Station Master I'Anson, taken in c.1910.

This huge piece of timber is seen being collected from Bakewell Station in 1906. It was about to be delivered to the church during the restoration of the roof.

Rowsley

Rowsley station on the extension to Buxton line started in 1860 and opened in 1867. The passengers are waiting for the Matlock train.

Bretton

Bretton Clough Farm. It was originally two farms, the left hand side being Hawley's Farm and the lower one being Fairest Clough House, dating from 1782.It was last occupied in 1919 and the roof was removed in 1935. The last occupant was Joseph Townsend who was quoted as saying that he had 'two houses and over 100 ackers o'land for forty pun a year rent, an' it were as dear as hell fire at that'. The lower scene shows the farm remains in c.1986.

Brough

Brough Mill is the building on the right. It was extended to the right in 1984. The horse has just come over the bridge, built in 1824. The mill was originally a water driven corn mill.

Buxton

OPPOSITE

This photograph is pre-1901 when the huge Empire Hotel was built behind and to the right of The Palace Hotel, seen in the mid-distance. Note the hot baths to the right of The Crescent; and the rear view of the Pump Room in front of The Crescent.

The Old Hall Hotel is on the left. The mid section with the two bays is in fact the original building bought by Bess of Hardwick's husband in 1571.

Between the hotel and The Crescent are the Natural Baths including the original thermal spring bath. Behind the left-hand end of the Crescent is the George Hotel, built in 1773 and purchased by the Duke of Devonshire by 1819.

It may have been Mr Dakeyne, who built the George, who refused to release land to the Duke to enable a larger crescent to be built. On the left is St John's Church, opened in 1811 and built at a cost of £6,758. The dome marks the Devonshire Hospital; to the right of it is The Palace Hotel, probably the largest hotel in the county. In the foreground are the Terrace Walks of 1817. The vases came from the Duke's house, Londesborough, in Yorkshire in that year.

On the far right are the two railway stations, the Midland railway being the nearest, with the LNWR Station (still open, but largely demolished) behind.

Station Approach to the twin stations, viewed from The Terrace. The far arcade stretched up to the Midland Railway Station. The advert on the side of Newbold's shop on the right, beyond The Grove Hotel reads: 'Newbold's Dressmaking & Millinery, Showrooms, Mantles, Special Corset House, Hosiery, Gloves'. The view dates from pre-1901.

The Pump Room & Terrace Walk behind it. The arches were subsequently filled in.

The interior of the Pump Room, with visitors taking a glass of mineral water.

The Buxton Hydro, a huge hotel in Hartington Street, built in 1866 and now demolished. It extended into the buildings behind the arch.

The Buxton Dairy shop in Dale Street.

The Buxton Dairy milk cart, decorated for a special (but unknown) event.

Clematis Drive, Buxton with a fine group of ladies dressed presumably for a Coronation celebration. In the top right-hand corner; you can just read 'To Brend...', which may recall a distant memory for some!

Ashford Dale on the A6.

Cat & Fiddle Inn

The Cat & Fiddle Inn on the Buxton-Macclesfield road. It clearly has been used to receiving guests on a trip out into the country for a long while.

Chapel-en-le-Frith

Old interior views of inns are uncommon but here are two postcard views of the Kings Arms Hotel in Chapel-en-le-Frith. They show the lounge and dining room.

The Market Place and former Packhorse Inn, Chapel-en-le Frith with the old cattle market.

Chapel Milton

Chapel Milton viaduct.

Chatsworth

Chatsworth and the Salisbury Lawns. The young yew trees have grown to the extent of masking the effect of the statues. These lawns have not been treated with fertiliser in over 200 years and are rich in low growing plants as a result.

Chinley

Chinley's earliest station, with at least five 'taxis' awaiting custom.

Cressbrook Mill

Two views taken on the same day showing the former cotton mill at Cressbrook in Monsal Dale. They show the old north-light-roofed extension at the front right, although it appears to be flat on the nearer view (both taken on the same day in the 1980s). The chimney has been demolished. The nearest, three-storey building is the original mill purchased by Sir Richard Arkwright. The pedimented building on the left survives as part of a redevelopment of the site as apartments.

Derwent Village

Derwent Valley prior to the construction of Ladybower Reservoir. The view is from above the former Grainsfoot Farm (above the girl's head) looking towards Crook Hill. Note the old packhorse road descending the hillside and heading for Derwent village.

Crossing Mill Brook at Derwent with the church off to the left. The path leads to the road where a left turn took you down the valley road to the Hall which would have been on your right. It is likely that these walkers were heading there when it was a youth hostel, for the photograph is in a selection which includes the Hall at that time.

Derwent Hall, showing the garden front (facing south) and the chapel at the end.

The river frontage (facing west).

The river frontage again plus the rear side of the house. The photographer is taking a picture of 'Peeping Tom' (see below).

'Peeping Tom'. Today he is a resident of Castleton Hall youth hostel, purchased to replace Derwent Hall. The latter opened in 1931 and finally closed its doors in 1942.

Derwent village. The path leads to the Mill Brook footbridge (see p.23). The Hall is hidden by the trees behind the church. The latter was built in 1867. The date is cut into a stone photographed the last time the village was exposed by drought in the late 1980s (see inset).

Exposed remains of Derwent Hall with the chapel in the foreground. The water on the left is in the former pool in the garden with yew tree stumps beyond it. The building (usually under water) is a valve house on the water pipe from Derwent Reservoir. One can be seen in Hathersage behind houses south of the main through road. It has been exposed three times since the valley was flooded in the mid-1940s. The dip in the tree line marks the current road.

Derwent Valley

Howdon House Farm in the Upper Derwent Valley with what looks like ten sheep shearers at work.

This sheepwash was at Birchinlee Bridge, now under Derwent Reservoir.

A close up of the Birchinlee Bridge sheepwash with six men in the water by the bridge (which was also called Ouzelden Bridge).

During the construction of Derwent and Howden dams, upriver from the (later) Ladybower dam, a village was built for the many workers employed there. It was called Birchinlee. Here is Jesse Eyres mobile butcher's shop at Birchinlee. The building on the left is part of the Recreational Hall built in 1902.

One of the main Birchenlee village streets, looking towards the Recreational Hall. The little cabin is the sweet and tobacco shop.

Pay day at the Howden Reservoir construction site. The building is the Derwent Valley Water Board's offices.

The dams were built with stone brought up the valley from Grindleford to Bamford, where a branch-line was built up the Derwent Valley. This loco, French, was supplied new by Manning Wardle in 1902 and worked on the Derwent dam site.

Edensor

The former school at Edensor now demolished. Behind on the right is the church.

Errwood

From one inundated valley to another: this is Goytsbridge Farm now below Errwood Reservoir in the Goyt Valley.

The ruins of Errwood Hall in 1961.

Now demolished, this was the former Errwood Farm, just north of the road from Goyts Bridge to Pym Chair. It has the distinction of being one of the initial 11 youth hostels which opened at Easter 1931, the only one in the Peak District.

This suspension bridge existed over the Fernilee Reservoir until the road across the new Errwood Reservoir provided an alternative. It was downstream from Goyts Bridge.

Eyam

The annual sheep roast in Eyam, with a pile of oatcakes on the table.

This shows the former Ball Inn at the junction of Eyam Dale and Middleton Dale pre-1919. The lane up past the inn goes to Eyam village. The buildings have all been demolished.

RIGHT

Early in the last century it was found that the old lead mine tips on Eyam Edge included huge deposits of fluorspar, which had a value in the smelting of iron ore. It was exported from Liverpool to the USA, hence the names on the loco, known as the *Spar Queen*. Over 150,000 tons was excavated from around Miners Engine and Broadlow mines alone.

Later the *Spar Queen* was replaced by the steam traction engines (right) and petrol driven lorry (left),

Grindleford

These premises were the General Store and Post Office, at Grindleford, almost opposite the Sir William Hotel. The scene dates from the 1880s. It was run by R. Kenyon.

Another view of the same property, complete with a two-wheeled trap.

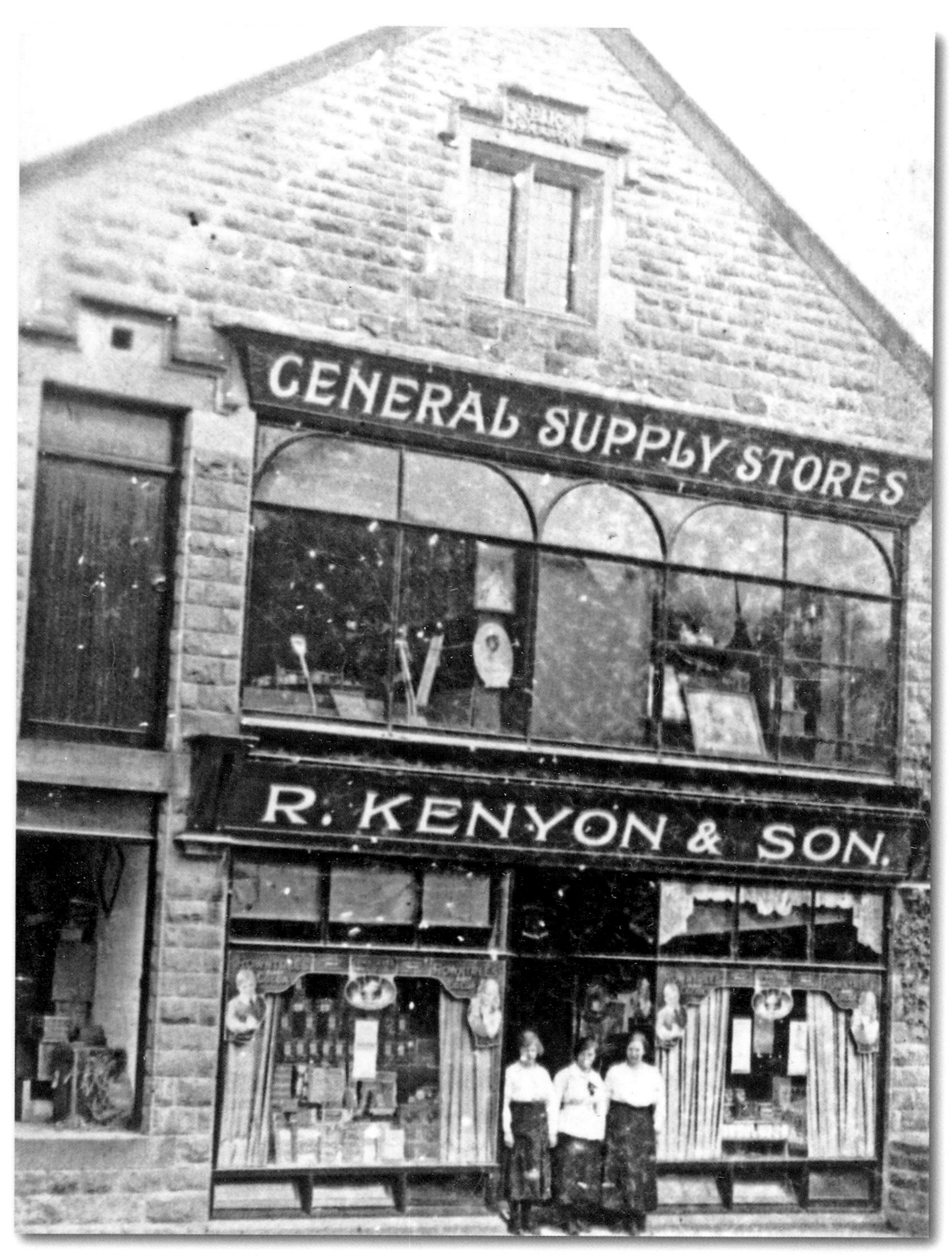

The General Store moved across the road when this property was built in c. 1914 adjacent to the Sir William Hotel. Kenyon's went into liquidation and the premises were later used as a bakers and café. In 1972 it was demolished and the land used as the hotel car-park. Seen are Peter Kenyon's three daughters.

Grindleford railway station shortly after it opened in 1898 following the completion of Totley tunnel (adjacent). It shows Mr Kenyon's horse buses. The premises are now a very popular café.

Building The Maynard Inn in Grindleford in 1908 on land owned by the Maynard family.

The Kenyon's also hired out this coach, looking resplendent in this view.

Lead Mill Bridge, Grindleford. This area has seen significant development since this scene was taken.

Blue John Stone

This is a remarkable photograph showing J W Puttrell's Blue John collection. It shows vases, urns, a table, a section through a large piece of the ornamental stone etc. Unfortunately, the building housing the display received a direct hit from a German bomber, destroying the collection.

Odin Lead Mine, Castleton

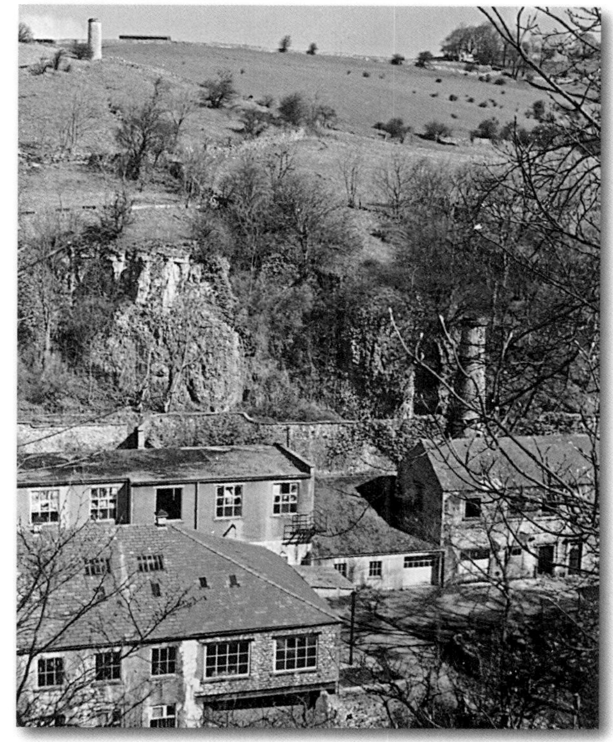

ABOVE

Blue John stone is located only at Castleton. Here is a view of Odin Mine at Castleton, situated close to the Blue John Mine above the trees. Note Mam Tor, the Shivering Mountain, in the background. This mine entrance no longer exists. In the foreground is a jig tub for separating lead ore in water.

Litton Mill, below Millers Dale

LEFT

Following its closure, a view of the former cotton mill showing it in a derelict condition.

Longdendale

Two views of the railway line after closure. The electric cable has been removed, probably because of its value. These views were taken at Crowden. The road to the left goes to Glossop.

Millers Dale

Ex-Midland Railway Loco 0-6-0 No. 58224, built in 1883. She is seen in September 1955, shortly before she was withdrawn, at Millers Dale Station.

Monsal Head

A loco about to cross the viaduct at Monsal Head.

Another scene of a loco just having crossed Monsal Head viaduct.

Sparrowpit

A carnival outside The Wanted Inn, Sparrowpit on Peace Day 1918. The Great War ended at the 11th hour of the 11th day of the 11th month of 1918.

Stoney Middleton

A play in progress at Stoney Middleton.

Tideswell

The former Kings Head was demolished to open up the view of the church, the entrance gates being just visible to the right. The road has now been widened too. The pub sold Tennant's ales and stouts and the licensee was Thomas Needham. It was opposite The Bulls Head.

This may have been taken for propoganda purpose. The infantry are recruiting volunteers for the relief of Mafeking in 1900 outside the now demolished Kings Head pub. The churchyard railings may be seen in the background.

Tideswell and District Co-op shop in the 1950s. Note the Ford Popular car and the milk churns.

Wardlow Mires

Watergrove lead mine chimney in 1960, prior to its demolition. It was built in 1837 and was 80ft high. It was situated at the top of Middleton Dale on the road to Wardlow Mires.

Whaley Bridge

RIGHT
Junction of the Cromford and High Peak Railway with the line to Whaley Bridge station.

BELOW
The Whaley Bridge incline on the Cromford and High Peak Railway which ended at Whaley Bridge Wharf on the Peak Forest Canal.

New and Current Local Titles

Visiting Britain's Heritage: The Peak District
Lindsey Porter
96pp; full colour; £9.99 ; paperback
ISBN: 978 1 84306 520 3
Details main features of the area's rich heritage expressed through buildings; prehistoric remains; road, canal & railways; historic visitor attractions. Over 70 sites included. **Spring 2011**

Memories of a Moorland Farmer
Len Ward
c. 64pp; mono; £7.99; paperback; well illustrated
ISBN: 978 1 84306 521 0
The late Len Ward wrote details of his life in a flowing and moving account. His world has gone for ever. He started school getting there in a pony and trap he purchased, aged 6, from his farm wages. He left his pony in a field behind Upper Elkstones School until home-time, when he started work.

Lost Houses of North Staffordshire
Cath Walton & Lindsey Porter
160pp; mono; £14.99; paperback; 200 illustrations
ISBN: 978 1 84306 195 3
A reprint of this lovely book, featuring nearly 100 former country seats and other houses, many of which no longer survive.

Alton Towers Past & Present
Michael Fisher
192pp; mono; £12.99; paperback;
ISBN: 978 1 84306 409 1
A thoroughly researched history of this huge house reduced now to a shell. 'A scholarly piece of architectural and social history written with passion'. Times Literary Supplement.

LANDMARK COLLECTOR'S LIBRARY
BYGONE
STAFFORDSHIRE
MOORLANDS

Lindsey Porter

Bygone Staffordshire Moorlands
Lindsey Porter
96pp; mono; £9.99; paperback
ISBN: 978-1-84306-471-8
Over 170 images of days gone by in the Staffpordshire Moorlands (but excluding the town of Leek). It includes a chapter on railways of the Churnet Valley

LANDMARK COLLECTOR'S LIBRARY
BYGONE DAYS
IN THE SOUTHERN
DERBYSHIRE DALES

Lindsey Porter

Bygone days in the Southern Derbyshire Dales
Lindsey Porter
48pp; mono; £4.99; paperback
ISBN: 078-1-84306-527-2
Companion to this book, covering the area of Hartington – Matlock and south of there

available from all good book shops and Horizon Press
☎ 01335 347349 or email books@thehorizonpress.co.uk